Lead Generation

B. Vincent

Published by RWG Publishing, 2021.

While every precaution has been taken in the preparation of this book, the publisher assumes no responsibility for errors or omissions, or for damages resulting from the use of the information contained herein.

LEAD GENERATION

First edition. July 28, 2021.

Written by B. Vincent.

Also by B. Vincent

Bridge Pages
Business Acquisition
Business Bogging
Marketing Automation
Better Meetings
Conversion Optimization
Creative Solutions
Employee Recruitment
Startup Capital
Employee Mentoring
Servant Leadership
Human Resources
Team Building
Freelancing
Funnel Building
Geo Targeting
Goal Setting
Immanent List Building
Lead Generation

Table of Contents

Lead Generation

Welcome to this seminar on lead age. In this course, we will cover how to gather leads and fabricate your rundown. This course is separated into three modules. Module one covers lead magnets, module two covers point of arrival plan, module three covers traffic and improvement. When this course is finished, you'll realize how to adequately dispatch lead age crusades, and make monstrous development for your business.

So moving right along, how about we jump into the principal module. Alright folks, welcome to module one. In this module, our master will show you lead magnets, and how to make the best ones for your business. So prepare to take a few notes, and how about we hop directly in.

Module One

So in this exercise, we will go over the various sorts of lead magnets you can use for lead age, so I will stroll through certain instances of conceivable lead magnets, and afterward we will go make our own little model for this course. So beginning basically costly finish of the range, as some may say, we have a little PDF report. These are truly normal and I'm certain you've seen around 1,000,000 of them on the web. In case you're on a limited spending plan or a tight timetable. These are an extraordinary method to convey a smidgen of significant worth as a trade-off for some select in. Here we have another PDF guide or digital book. Furthermore, the extraordinary thing about these is that you can in a real sense re-appropriate the substance keeping in touch with a consultant or authorized pre-composed materials somewhere else in the event that you can't be tried to make your own without any preparation. One disadvantage of the old digital book cut PDF model, obviously, is that they have low seen esteem, which can in some cases mean lower select in rates and less invigorated possibilities.

The following stage up could be something like a video course. Here we see a heap of two video courses being offered as a lead magnet. For a many individuals, this will have more seen esteem than the PDF document. So there's a basic way for you to acquire or make video content, or even repurpose your text based substance into video structure. That may assist with raising your apparent worth. Moving considerably further toward that path, we have a full enrollment and Academy with a huge load of video exercises and courses. As you can envision, this will be viewed as lovely significant for a free lead magnet.

Lastly, here we have kind of a heap of three video courses in addition to an enrollment. This is truly pushing the apparent worth of lead magnet as far as possible. So we should feel free to begin creating our own lead magnet. Presently clearly this exercise won't show you how to make the real substance that is something you or your organization need to do. So I'm not demonstrating how to compose a book, what we will do is accept that you've effectively made the actual substance, either by you or re-appropriating it to somebody or procuring it and authorizing it, and we will bundle it into an appealing lead magnet.

So we should come on here to my ecover maker.com. Also, suppose, we need to offer an aide on DIY home improvement. So how about we pick one of the tablet alternatives, way down here. That is consistently a cool method to address a digital book or a PDF guide, and we should set our experience on this to dark. How about we take a little title in here. Perhaps DIY home fix guide. How about we resize that a smidgen and move it around.

Presently we need a convincing picture. So how about we come here and we should type in, development. This will give us a huge load of results to browse. What's more, we should go with this one here, we'll bring that into our Ecover and reposition it a smidgen. When we're content with the manner in which it looks. We'll hit settle and we'll give it a couple of seconds to deliver that for us.

Okay, not awful. So we have an alluring lead magnet made here. Furthermore, the subsequent stage will be to introduce it in an alluring manner on the real greeting page, which is the thing that we'll cover in the following exercise.

Module Two

Hello people, welcome to module two. In this module, our master will tell you the best way to plan your point of arrival, so prepare to take a few notes, and how about we hop directly in.

Okay so here we are we will make our real presentation page. Presently, these are now and again alluded to as lead pages, points of arrival, select in pages, information exchange pages, crush pages, they're known all in all part of things. We will utilize Instapage for this cycle, however the standards apply to any greeting page programming and the interaction will be pretty much the equivalent paying little heed to which one you pick. So we'll begin by picking a layout. The smartest option is to keep things pretty moderate, moderate as could really be expected, to support select ins. So we're searching for something with a feature, perhaps a sub-feature, and obviously a structure that is practically it. Presently this one down here with an image of a house looks very great and it appears to accommodate our theme really well which is home fix in the event that you review, how about we go with this one. So inside the editorial manager here, I'll start by erasing every one of the additional parts that we needn't bother with.

Presently we should will work, changing the duplicate. Suppose at last dominated the craft of DIY home improvement and fix. That sounds great to me. We should move that up a smidgen, and we will require some space to embed our E cover from the past exercise directly beneath that.

When that E covers in there we'll change the catch text. Get the aide ought to be acceptable. Furthermore, well off, that is essentially it. Our pages looking very great. Before we finish, however, we'll need to associate it to our autoresponder programming. So we can really begin fabricating our email list. Whenever that is done, our page is prepared to begin taking care of some traffic, which is the thing that we'll cover in the following exercise.

Module Three

Okay, welcome to module three. In this module, our master will show you traffic strategies and streamlining your lead age crusade. So prepare to take a few notes, and we should hop directly in.

Okay, folks, so we're simply going to momentarily address two of the most well-known traffic sources, specifically, Google and Facebook advertisements, and afterward we will get into the fundamentals of investigating and upgrading your mission execution. So for one thing, Facebook promotions are clearly a very notable type of publicizing, and they're consistently utilized by organizations for lead age. There's an assortment of configurations to browse, large numbers of which you've presumably seen yourself according to a customer point of view, commonly. There's photograph or picture advertisements, there's video promotions, there's merry go round advertisements that contain different pictures or recordings, there's slideshow promotions, assortment advertisements which can be utilized to grandstand numerous items, and even courier promotions which are getting very famous nowadays. The catchphrase to remember here is local. This is the thing that has made Facebook advertisements so powerful. They figured out how to make your advertisements look like they're simply aspect of the natural Facebook experience, they look and feel pretty much like individual posts like things that have a place on Facebook, consequently the word local.

Presently straight up there with Facebook is Google AdWords. Also, the foundation of AdWords is their hunt advertisements. How might you want to put your advertisements directly before individuals at the specific second, they're quite looking for your answer. That's right, that is the thing that you're doing here, you're basically paying to have your item, put directly at the highest point of Google's outcomes pages. These are staggeringly amazing, incredible promotions, and an extraordinary method to drive traffic. Whenever you have that traffic coming in, however, you should have the option to measure and comprehend your lead page's presentation. So we should discuss how to do that. Here we have an investigation page within our point of arrival programming. We're ready to screen all the fundamental information we need to think about our page, similar to the number of guests are we getting, the number of those guests are picking in and becoming leads. What's the change rate? What's the presentation resemble extra time or on certain days? Are there any patterns? So for this one, we have an incredible transformation rate. We've had 281 guests who have gone to the page and out of that 177 have selected in through that pick in structure, which gives us an astounding transformation pace of 63%, that is 63% of guests who go to the page, and select in and join our rundown, that is awesome. This is significant information since it makes our publicizing efforts unsurprising. At the point when we're deciding how much cash to spend on driving traffic, we have a rough thought of the number of leads, every dollar of promotion spend, will get us, which is colossally helpful when running efforts. This information is particularly helpful down here in case you're parted trying different greeting pages. Allow me to show you what I mean. Examine this hitting the fairway lead page. What's more, presently, view this one. It couldn't be any more obvious, they're by and large something similar. You can run a similar measure of traffic to each page, and afterward utilize those details we were simply taking a gander at to figure out which one proselytes better. What's more, in all honesty, a straightforward difference behind the scenes picture or even words in the feature or the shade of a catch, can cause a tremendous distinction in execution, split testing things like that can save you a ton on publicizing. Here's an illustration of a lead page with a three-way split test, where the solitary thing that changed was the foundation picture. Examine the distinction here.

Presently, even the least performing page actually has a quite decent change rate here, however goodness, take a gander at the top-performing variety, practically 80%. What we can do now is simply begin piping most or even the entirety of our traffic to that varieties as far as we might be concerned's performing incredible, and we will improve value for our promoting money, and presently we are aware of a specific component, for this situation, a foundation picture that seems to support high changes, which may prove to be useful for future lead pages and even deals pages. So that is it folks, we've effectively gone through the entire interaction of setting up and enhancing a lead age mechanical assembly.

Don't miss out!

Visit the website below and you can sign up to receive emails whenever B. Vincent publishes a new book. There's no charge and no obligation.

https://books2read.com/r/B-A-QWUO-TTUQB

BOOKS 2 READ

Connecting independent readers to independent writers.

Also by B. Vincent

Affiliate Marketing
Affiliate Marketing
Affiliate Marketing

Standalone
Affiliate Recruiting
Business Layoffs & Firings
Business and Entrepreneur Guide
Business Remote Workforce
Career Transition
Project Management
Precision Targeting
Professional Development
Strategic Planning
Content Marketing
Imminent List Building
Getting Past GateKeepers
Banner Ads
Bookkeeping

Bridge Pages
Business Acquisition
Business Bogging
Marketing Automation
Better Meetings
Conversion Optimization
Creative Solutions
Employee Recruitment
Startup Capital
Employee Mentoring
Servant Leadership
Human Resources
Team Building
Freelancing
Funnel Building
Geo Targeting
Goal Setting
Immanent List Building
Lead Generation

About the Publisher

Accepting manuscripts in the most categories. We love to help people get their words available to the world.

Revival Waves of Glory focus is to provide more options to be published. We do traditional paperbacks, hardcovers, audio books and ebooks all over the world. A traditional royalty-based publisher that offers self-publishing options, Revival Waves provides a very author friendly and transparent publishing process, with President Bill Vincent involved in the full process of your book. Send us your manuscript and we will contact you as soon as possible.

Contact: Bill Vincent at rwgpublishing@yahoo.com www.rwgpublishing.com

I used to stand in a corner of the square at this time ev
offer my condolence and love to my dead brother, Kai. I have t
silence without any flowers and candles. Everyday at this hour of
I know that some eyes are always on me watching.   They are de

I'm Shin Li, 45 years lives in Beijing   and a doc
comparative literature from Peking University and presently a
teacher in Tsinghua. My husband is a surgeon in in the state ho
our family is like other city families where fights and togetherr
hand in hand and more precisely we lead more or less a decent
the four walls. Our kids are already grown-ups and doing the
studies in UK. But my family is always worried about me of
reason which I couldn't shake off even if I had tried hundred
times. To my husband it could jeopardise my very existence one
if they all surround me with all the protective shield they h
could I deny my undefying relation with my brother, Kai   kill
Tinanmen Square Protests in the year 1989! I had a blood rela
him which is very close and that grew intense after his death. H
more alive to me after I understand him well much after his dea
too young then when all that happened.

My husband knew all about it and everything to him as
daylight. I had not hidden anything from him. After we d
engaged one day I told him : "Zao, would you be able to marry
apprehending that I could be jailed or executed of being bloodi
with my brother ? The MSS are watching me all the time. They
me in the dungeon on any pretext. Life would then become toug
They could implicate you also for me. " Hearing me with upright
fiancé or better to say my husband at present gave me a warm
whispered through my ears " We'll tell them to keep us in a si
Out of passion I kissed him with all my strength and we fucke
first time.

My dad was a pharmacist and my mother a dedicated
who cared for everything in the house- animate and inani
brother a good student was studying engineering in the coll

se words when my brother was telling one of his friends. Kai
sensitive to his studies and to everyone surrounded him. But I
at all of a sudden the number of bicycles parked outside our
 increasing day after day and friends of my brother began
. I used to ask my mother " I'll also have so many friends when
my brother's age." Mom smiled at me and got herself busy in
 chores. Outside the police patrolling began frequent in the
olic squares and in the front of every government buildings – all
 while going to my school with my friends. It never occurred to
the changes happening so fast around us. To be frank, I was
atured enough to sense those goings-on that could turn into a
assacre and that would lead to a perpetual loss to my family. I
rother in that most gruesome massacre which our leaders of the
ave successfully covered up by fear tactics and severe brutality.
 present time try to smoke it off or even try to talk about it in
d come under the strict surveillance of MSS who could cut him
ely without much noise.

steps on the wooden stairs of our house became more and
lding day after day and sometimes stamped on till midnight.
nes in and whisk off after having talks and gossips with my
 closed door which sometimes blasted off and heard " This
t regime should be replaced by democracy. They began
g us, scaring us with their machine guns and tankers, but we'll
d to this." Eventually the combined voice, a bit louder to the
e spurted out , "Yes, yes, we'll". Often I asked my mother
that's happening around which was not witnessed before, my
ed to say that my brother and his companions are trying to
ew day in China that would be completely different from what
ow. Being a child of ten years I lacked such understandability

only inanimate thing I adored at those days of my years was
- I used to take great care of it, a birthday gift from my father,
or school and back home, short distances were easily covered
 considered it as one my of my best friends. At an essay writing
ss when I was asked to write down about my best friend, I
ny bicycle and described the movable metallic object with
 subtlities that created squeaking laughter in the class. The
named me for a while but I remain unfazed. Whenever

All of a sudden my father came home and told me not to
the bicycle from the next day as the tension outside was mou
Authorities were barricading roads and lanes to put up a hard p
around Beijing against a probable riotous demonstration, the po
taking all the safety measures to resist any kind of disruptic
public life- all were prerequisities for stopping any klnd of unla
as they used to call that episode even now. It was evening wh
sipping down a hot soup and and my brother, Kai was not in th
might have not returned from his college. Schools would rema
and there should be heavy patrolling in the streets, even mili
there in the streets to tackle any kind of worse situation. As far a
recollect spring was almost over summer was approaching and
would be the middle of May. The heat of the summer began bu
skin and beads of perspiration were surfacing on the foreheads,
armpits. Overexhaustion making us tired and sleepy but the
outside was becoming grim and moving towards a flashpoint.

Near Muxidi students and people of pro-democracy wings
on a hunger strike and the word hunger-strike didn't make insic
that age. I asked my father out of curiosity "Papa, how could th
the hunger? Are they really doing it?" Hearing me, my dad brea
with spilling laughter but after sometime soothed down my q
elegance- "Shin, hunger strike means not to take food or any ed
like fasting. And they are doing to turn the authorities to listen
You'll understand it when you'll grow up." Yes, it's true now
enough and wild too, to sense those words and the nasty
operations carried out by the Army and the police against the
their own country on that fateful day. It whirred out so fast a
strict control and surveillance that every demonstrating circles v
deterred and throttled.

I made to live in this country without my choice because
that I would not be able to move out as the people of MSS is wat
round the clock. My every moves are monitored and even my
closely surveilled. My brother died in 1989 massacre, i.e., about
ago but I was still living a prisoner's life because of being sang
related to my brother .Sometimes this thought ails me te
crawling sensation run down through my spine forcing me to the
no-return. "Why am I considered hostile to my country? Why ar

brother runs over my eyes which relieved me from those
d whys.

netimes sudden fits carried me over and I was shrouded under
nist of ill-thoughts and suicidal urges, thanks to those Buddhist
ad them– rescue me from the impending attacks , lead me
shining and glorious aura. The writings inside those texts aids
over those lonely crisis I seldom used to go through. Not being
o but I go by the concept of godliness that emblazoned by truth
Though my country has no state religion but to my knowledge
many leaders and persons at the top of Communist Party lead a
ne religious life away from the eyes of their own watchdogs. I
article on this subject titled "Believe in false beliefs" in my
magazine but was abruptly rejected on the filmy pretext of
wordy. While being talked to the members of the magazine
e they had not offered me a good reason, even they fear to
th the issue like someone watching them from behind or from
sniper. In this country if you are noisy against the regime you're
eep worse than the hell – there's no option for you to deal with
u've to go by the flow or keep yourself distant from all the
of the government. Injustice, forced labour, false trials leads to
ions are all the things that are rampant inside a closed watchful
-even the wind dares to carry them out in the open.

s threatened verbally a number of times and I was told if I try
a noise about my brother's death or if try to do anything
in their eyes the consequences would not be pleasing for me.
was really upset with me about this and I always tried to keep
away from this but I know that they could ride up to any
or descend down to the downest causing physical and
ical inflictions to anyone related to me that forces me to confess
committed a crime or a sin beyond any doubts. Meanwhile I
eep myself inside a non-vocal shell that helps me to pen down
nts in a diary that I keep in a hidden closet. One day I would
t them published in some foreign publishing house when my
ill be settled and my body would be immune to any kind of
nt even the scaring death.

is the only prop of my life to live the days ahead, I really don't

me. Perhaps the worst I thought of. My husband and I had talked
of this but could not reach into any well-founded solution. The onl
get relieved of all my worries- I used to go across the banks of
and sat down by it, outpours all the tears upon the flowing waters

My brother's death was really a sudden blow to our fan
father- a dauntless pro-democratic had managed to cope up
death of his son considering it as a martyr's one but my mother n
inconsolable till her last breath which finally took away her s
mind. In a middle of a night in a mental asylum my mother brea
for the last time and that was long after my father's death. A n
had the ability to enclose his sorrows and anguish into his he
finest elegance had also succumbed to the misery rubbing his te
in loneliness. I saw my father struggling every night inside th
doors but he didn't lose his mind like my mother. The passing
my brother and my mother's consequent insanity had weake
from inside but he went on with his life hiding away his sorrov
under the flesh and blood till his end. He was also watched by
but he didn't care or afraid of them. Donned with bravery he piss
off silently and intelligently. His normal life had not been distu
damaged by the sadful events he had passed through. During the
my father was a bit dishevelled but it didn't last longer and I saw
quickly he slipped into his habitual doings like a mechanical robot.

My mother used to cry almost everytime but her tears rain
profusely when she stood by the photo of my brother hung on th
our living room- smiling, ecstatic and freeness spun around him.
there with my mother as she felt him almost everywhere surrou
The sorrow in her heart for her dead son could not be brought
words but left alone to be felt only.

The day was almost cloudy when we were anxious at the
waiting for my brother but it looked morbidly strange- nor
friends frequenting our house came by. Only the sirens of the pc
and military vans were heard defeaning the eerie silence surrou
And my father was sure at " None will come, those who are alive
the country or gone underground and the rest are dead or will be
till death. The Communist regime had even barred the foreign n
and newsmakers from entering Beijing. They barricaded the er

kes his way back then we've to assume he's no more. He's
My father could not resist his emotional outburst – banged the
inks of the door with his furious fists.

ouple of days had passed off. I was not matured enough to
nd what has happened and what was still going on around the
I was clear in one thing that something very bad had fretted
ooking at the roads piled under burnt remains, fumes from them
ing, blood stains almost in every pavements, few people who
ering outside   were under severe trauma and disoriented ,
nells of bullets lying on the asphalt tracks, army was still
 – Beijing seemed to have been   drowned into an abyss of
 The animated pace of the city was lost replaced by a morbid
ashen one. Only the undaunted Army was reigning wide across
 glaring in their eyes. They were out to beat and kill everyone
 against the regime regardless of her or his age and sex. Like
less sun in the summer the Army was there to monitor, thwart
 out the democratic impressions. They were already done but
kely that they were yet to finish- they only crossed half the

 were almost sure that Kai was dead and waiting for the
ion. Out of swelling distress my mother had ran out a couple of
 somehow my father had been able to turn her back like a
 child not willing to go to school. Years went by. She later
herself into a state of lunacy that took away her life wretchedly
d. My father lived a life only for me and I was able to learn that
as a bit older. I saw how my father had taken the place of my
hen she was almost out of her mind and had done those family
 great pains to keep the family tree alive. I also saw my father
p and down inside his room like a rangy animal seeking shelter
ort. It occurred seldom but I experienced those things so close
 every reasons to hate the regime and to see the regime going
 other Communist regimes in the world. To see China in a
y where every Chinese could talk freely and raise their voice
he wrongs of the regime is my only dream. But many of my
 and friends used to taunt my dream as hallucination which
ver become true. But the words of Martin Luther King " I had a
" often rang into my ears that keeps my dream alive with me.

while making demonstrations or revolts against the wrongs. M
died of cardiac arrest and I had not to witness his death since I w
from Beijing and in Shanghai with my scholarship. The news car
while I was travelling in a city bus but I didn't cry out in sponta
was shaken a little but I went straight to my hostel took off my
boarded the train and headed towards Beijing to ritualise my
last rites. While on his last rites I realised how my father h
cowardly for me not doing anything but accepting his son's mu
other common events. It was a murder, a murder indeed comn
the state by the Communist regime as they did against all th
raised their voice for democracy during the June incidents. Hea
deep sighs my father consoled himself by saying " You can't do
against them, they've weapons in their hands, they've power,
everything they have to put you down forever." He even advisee
to ruin my life running after my brother's death. And I also
anguish and qualms buried deep inside me in a secret closet. C
will blow it off like bomber or perhaps a cracker that maybe I
whisked away by the wind- but I will do it for the departed so
brother.

Three long years had passed after the expiry of my fath
kept my head down to the books completing my doctorate whi
enable me for a decent livelihood. My fiance was at that time a
in surgery and we met laughed exchanged pleasantries and often
I find him a very well-behaved, suave and a practical man – not-
looking but he has air of elegance around which makes h
charming. I never thought of marrying him because he did
anything about me nor do I but we both felt a strong inrush towa
other. Perhaps that entwined us both from inside and led us to r
Raising a family had never hit me in any way neither I thought
deeply but I found it a rescue to my solitary living. I agreed
fiance's proposal and we married without any pre-conditions.

After a week passed I told my husband everything a
disaster my family had faced for my brother's revolt against the
He heard my untold story intently without breaking into the mi
for a once. "It happened to every family of Beijing mostly."- I
out finally. Perhaps he was right miseries lies within the four
every domestic household just like us without any impressions.

ighfare where foreign tourists often asked the guides about the
and in response they keep themselves mum or say " It's
Please don't ask."

2

It was a rainy night. My father had just came back
work and was preparing his tea as he used to. He lived alone a
some days off from my studies and came to visit him. He was g
but unfortunately there no one around to take care of him. So
come and visit him regularly which he also didn't like as he vie
my visits could hamper my regular studies. But I never used to
his words in this matter particularly and he also knew that as wel

"How are your studies?"- He asked me while sip
steaming tea.

"Its fine, papa. How's your health?" I enquired.

"Ok. Old age always has problems. If you're not busy
going to tell you something."- his voice grew serious.

I turned back at him and told -"Not so, papa. Please

"Do you want to know how your brother's life ended?

His words pricked my ears hard and I closed the bc
hand putting all my attention to him. He looked up at me and
the untold story.

" It was few days after June 4. The entire city was
under military crackdown but somehow I managed to go to Za
through lanes and bylanes, one of your brother's close friends t
about Kai's whereabouts. His father and his mother were also in
distress like us waiting for their son's comeback. Zao's father
strong took my hands and let me inside before I was rounded
military or by the police. Zao's father was a professor and an
person but didn't approve Zao's ways of going against the admir
He differed angrily. He believed that the students, workers
demonstrators were not united at all and they were ide
disconnected and also didn't have proper plans to move ahead
agenda or manifesto. What they planned was to dislodge the pe
were in power and replace it by democratic system could not be
with the way they had chosen. They hadn't made any dialogues
government before demonstrating. They simply walked into th
raised their voices which simply means going into a war wit
artillery. Listening to his lecture I became bored and with
discontent I asked him about his son and he cried down like a

en I saw some military personnel a bit far away clobbering a
. The young man was crying wriggling and trying to stop them
ail wounded hands but they kept on beating him until they put a
his head. They fired at him like a mangy dog. Watching the
a dense cold sweat ran down over me which was about to
e off but somehow I managed to get over and fled off from

voice grew feebler as if he could not speak further- his stony
so. Quickly I ran upto him and offered my rescuing hand to
feel better and tide over the hiccup. He rested down his head
and tried to smile but tears replaced it like a sudden change in
er. My eyes also became moistened and our sorrows for the first
ed together for sometime. It was evening - darkness had
rough. Streets outside lit up and night came in a trolley of
ses. My father hadn't finished the story and he would tell me
elt like-I thought so. He went to his room and I began to get
oks for the approaching semesters.

r a few days my father came up to me and I sensed from his
hat he wanted to finish the remaining part of the tragedy.
books and everything I had in my hand as I was upto to the
y nerves to know the tragic end of my brother. Helping my
somehow straddled up in front of me and began from where
I knew he had a good memory and he didn't need to be
.

hin a few more days I could manage to rummage the entire city
ully but unable to trace Kai or his whereabouts. And that made
resolute and stubborn and I began exploring different many
et to him- alive or dead at the end of the day . It became
for me as well since I became almost certain that he could
e since he had no means to leave this country. If he failed to
st have surely been killed by those butchers just like the boy I
hile leaving his friend's house. Many of his friends were killed
ne and some were disappeared like Kai. Who knows where they
ped or fled ? Sometimes igniting thoughts provoked me to
nachine gun from a soldier and killed one of them just they had

showered at them like pesticides. He also added that no one
from that lashing fire. The demonstrators first thought rubbe
sprayed on them to disperse but when they saw people falling u
one another they ran amuck. But none survived from the deadly
And all those news had made me more adamant in finding Ka
might he be no more but as a father I had every right to see
mortal remains. Going to the authority would do no good
become risky and the only way left was to ....". He could not
line, tears bathed down his wrinkled cheeks that melted awa
strength making him look helpless and miserable. I ran up to him
him feel at ease rubbing his shoulders and back. Within a short
got back himself into normalcy gulping down a glass of water ar
with a firmer voice than before.

" After a week or so I heard that the government had been
to bury a few hundred dead bodies clandenstinely in the outskir
from the eyes of the common people. Perhaps in darknes
midnight hours. I began using all my connections to get every
information on this. And nothing of all these things I told to you
as you could sense why. When I was at all my mind to get tov
son presumably dead the police and the military started punishi
families who werc trying to trace the infidels- they began to cal
that way because the government was in a run to save the
already been done in killing hundreds of innocent unarmed demo
and students. Kin Lai one of your brothers friend living a few ya
from here was also missing after that day and his parents
collective gesture of protesting in a silent way. They stood in th
at the dead end of a night with a photo of his son and a candle be
to show their outrage. But within a short while the police c
dragged them away from there ruthlessly to somewhere from wh
didn't came back. This news hovered all over the city and the sa
inflicted to everyone who tried to embarrass the governmen
manner they felt right. And those things were happening so fa
began to scare me and sometimes I thought of withdrawing my
my pursuit. I had responsibility for you and for your mother
anything happens to me the family which was in misery v
completely crippled and then wiped out without any trace.
thoughts begun threatening me like nightmares. But in some corr

themselves of being getting caught by the police as the military police started defaming them as infidel families. Reports were me from different corners that the parents or the members of such family were taken away by the police and went missing who returned dared to speak out in the open of the tragedy as he torture they faced and suffered. But I know in our locality many young people went missing after that incident but none courage to tell or to discuss about it. They just forgotten their amily member like a visiting stranger- perhaps they could but as possible for me. How could I forget my boy whom I beget ? so complicated that sometimes my urge compromises with my week had already passed. The tough policing and militarising ened and I got the information. A mass burial would be coming outskirts- a few kilometres away from the airport. The place was cant with some scattered foliage and was perfectly chosen for nd work. Living in a country where leaders speak about lofty socialism and sad to say they were making preparations to dump es of their own young citizens. However, I made a plan to make of the place where the graveyard would be dug and the task be smooth enough when the prevailing condition at outside is and volatile. But to go there which is close to the present day ea and about thirty kilometres from here was a risky adventure ice and military were still making frequent patrols. Besides that, nsport was not in the streets. The government has tightened its where around Beijing as well as also in other parts. Imprisoning hom they believe suspicious or chaotic. The police and the ere ordered to nab any person appearing destructive or hostile fter the demonstration. Even the parents or the near ones of the disappeared men and women tried to do anything as a mark of nsidered as an outrage. They were sent to jail or killed secretly- all government sponsored killings that could not be called for e. Travelling a long distance of about thirty kilometres or more become impossible for me since the military and the police had up the streets and I had to make it fast since the information to me was from a very authentic source. The communicator informed me that the military personnel were very much onto al of those bodies as they started decaying and many of them ecomposed. The morgues had been full and place for keeping

the dead bodies to their families. This was where we lived - a
communist nation. A sense of overtemptness has rubbed all c
Bravely I went out disregarding your mother's cautions to get
place where Kai be possibly dumped. I wanted to see him for
time. "

I saw my father was in a non-stop mood and was eager to tel
everything and I didn't want to interrupt him either. Beca
unbothered listener I suffered a lot going through it but I was
My father started again gulping down a glass full of water.
" I had skipped plan of making a survey of the place and decided
the day of burial. There was a binocular your brother used to
outings and I wanted to make use of it. If I get near to the buria
might get caught and every harm would then be inflicted upon m
I would stay away from a few yards of the spot and watch ev
through that instrument. But I had no plans of getting there w
about as I said earlier eighteen miles from here. I was simply
through the blinds and sometimes rushing out to see if the patro
slowed down. Hours were left to make a rash decision which I ha
something was pulling me from back and you could easily un
that. It came to me as a boon the administration had lifted the
for some hours and that was what I was waiting for. I was pla
whisking off from the house and took to the streets durir
unpatrolled hours. Those off hours were between nine in the mor
six in the evening. I had a plan to work out. I wore a tattered sho
torn shirt and a dirty pyjamas which help me to look like a desti
beggar and I told your mother to be off for a day or two. It was
and the darkness of the clouds standstilled everywhere and I
house after a goodbye to your mom. She understood but didn't
which was readable from her vivid eyes. I went out and the stre
almost empty except some dogs in the lanes running berserk.
took the main street and began walking like a beggar marching
without any destination. My hair was unkempt every loose ends h
down covering my face my nails were full of dirt my legs much lil
my nails. I had stained myself with dust and ashes as much a
before leaving the house to get a look of a beggar or a vagrant. Y
know all these things because you're too little at that time. I
smoke. "

ke this papa. " I lit up his smoke and he fagged in the first one
d puffed out slowly making it a white snake in the air. Then he
me and began the talking.
u're using this brand. It's good one. I had walked over four
it's still dark. The first patrol I saw after making through the
bylanes came up to me all of a sudden like a thunder that
up and down. But I remain unnerved and kept on walking
oking them at their eyes. One of the soldiers walked forward
me – where was I going ? Lifted up my face I raised my finger
ed it towards his nose, seeing this the other soliders lauged
chorus. Then they left me passing out some words- Mad, old
ort of. I kept on walking towards my destination. I was happy to
ce the trick had been playing. But the fear of getting caught and
d was also with me. Whatever might come upto I would not be
nd kept on going till I catch the glimpse of Kai- my dead son.
ou find it grievous enough for a father to embroiled into such a
But that's my destiny my very ill-luck. After walking over
e miles the sun above had came out feebly and drizzle by then
ed. I was thirsty and a bottle of water there in my rugpack
r my shoulder had soothed me down. There was some bread
of soup prepared and handed me by your mother before I left
. After walking off some miles I sat down by the side of the
d and broke a few crumbs since I knew I would have to go with
rovision till evening. I had money but if I went to a hotel or a
for food eyes would fall on me and that could destroy
I had in my mind. So I had carried on cautiously before
joes wrong or out of my way. A person walks for his health and
king for my dead son to see his corpse. Sometimes while on the
ead turns into a red charcoal and tempts me to kill the police
ry who were responsible for killing my son. During those
ours every sensible and insensible thoughts crowding up inside
g me destructive at once . When the sun was almost overhead
and looked for a shelter to get some rest. Because I was only
ometres away from my desired place. So I took a little nap by
of the road under an oak tree probably. The tree had a
le shade beneath and I sat down cosily under it with my legs
forward and slowly I died down to sleep. More than an hour
s sleeping and suddenly a chaotic giggle shook me up. A dozen

their laugh. They stood around me and watching me like an ape
I loved their glances and after sometime carried on with my
again. I started walking again leaving them behind with a lot
because I had to be closer to the spot before the daybreak. When
was about to go down beyond the horizon I was almost at the clo
spot. But what I saw was really unimaginable. The place was
cleared and a large hole was dug which could be able to pile u
than two hundred corpses. I was really horrified to see that vile p
the same time shamed of being a citizen of this country. Sin
watching all from an elevated ground through the binocular w
unblurredly and clearly hitting my eyes. Evening had fallen and
darkened above. A downpour was imminent again and I had to d
the night since there was neither shade nor any canopy to shield
from rain.The military as well as the police cars and vans had arri
the pit and the place had already lit up by the headlights
vehicles. I was in a crawling state like a reptile with my binocula
eyes. About an hour passed a vehicle larger than a truck arri
dead bodies. The military and the police scudded the area like sni
I slowly crawled back down where their searchlights didn't trace
soon as the lights were put down I crawled back upwards again to
was and sighted the horrific thing I ever seen. They began dum
bodies inside the pit like dead dogs and cats and every police and
manning there had scarfed their noses with handkerchiefs wh
those bodies they were dumping had began decomposing or alre
decomposed. The corpses were off-loaded so quickly from the tru
couldn't locate the face of Kai. It was all Kais dumping into the p
that way as my vision from that elevation viewed likewise. Jo
upto there for my son had made me somewhat selfish, my son
only been killed there were a lot of Chinese boys shot and kill
their parents had no information of them so to me I became
father of those innocent young victims or you could say martyrs
journey to my dead son oh sorry to my dead sons ends here. I ca
from there safely without a scratch and narrated the story to you
who understood but keep on asking me in a bickering way –
didn't find Kai. I failed to lead her into my path of thinking
result overthinking of Kai drove her to insanity. It's my fau
couldn't protect your mother, I took the responsibility. I failed to
calmness she needed during those overwrought times."

ing out of myself from misery I hurried up and offered him a
troke of my hands over his wrinkled face and balded head. We
each other in the most affectionate embrace that a daughter
 expect from his father or a father could only offer to his
aughter in such times. That warmest touch of affection could
usand miseries melt away.

to three days left to get back to Peking since my exams were
aching. But I was leaving with an overburdened soul wounded
ry of a massacre that surfaced in my country where my borther
like a stray animal and dumped secretly into an unknown pit. I
w whether taking away lives by the government whom our lives
on was an act of crime or be termed as an austere measure.
ot be crushed on any excuse be it a governmental misgiving or
nocide. But here there are many Tiananmen Mothers' who are
to speak out in public of their miseries and lamentations. It is
ed. How can a government censor a mother's breastbeating on
 of his son whom she lost at his green age! It's censored
he government is afraid of facing the consequences of the
people. Could any mother in the world remain unmourned after
of his only son? Could any mother be reticent when she find her
nocent kid was killed mercilessly? But to my mother the
crept in seated deeply inside her, battered her, crushed her
er and made her dismal before everyone.

a late afternoon while I was back from my high school I found
at home in a tizzy which was unusual to me since he used to
k after the evening fall. A neighbour called up my dad on
 to rescue my mother who was running wayward in a
manner. Neighbours knew about my mother's mental state but
she was found almost naked in the lane shouting out "Kai,
eatedly as he was looking out for him crazily. The grief heaped
 her grew enormous and that had completely subsided her
 Day after day she became violent and furious even to us who
r to comfort her from frenzy state. It was from that day our
nd helplessness manifolded and that went beyond the limits of
t. I saw often my father sat in his chair with hands covered his
gling all alone without any prop. Looking up at me sometimes in

slowly in front of my lucid eyes which intensified more du
absence of my father who remained out of Beijing mostly o
Consequently as a teenager I had to face the entire brunt of my
disorientations and mental sickness which sometimes tempted m
from the house but some invisible pull set me back to my place.
she used to wail and talk alone in front of Kai's photo which la
some minutes and then it lingered for hours and then after some
when her wailings became almost unstoppable. It stopped only w
was exhausted and dropped down to sleep. Since our house was a
we could easily manage to lock her into a room which was aw
mine to avoid noise that was not helpful for my studies. Whe
stepping to move into the college one day my father came into r
all of a sudden and told me that he decided to shift my mother
nearest asylum. She would be shifted the next morning. The
slapped me hard of not seeing my mother any more in the hous
she nursed me, fed me, pampered me and governed me with all
care. The decision to sancturise my mother was also log
reasonable as it was getting harder for us to manage my mother
activities that became more and more uncontrollable. We we
deep pressure in this matter as my father who was about to re
already devoted one-third of his life in taking care of his insa
precisely after Tiananmen massacre. Looking at a glance anyone
how tired and wasted away he was- the thick dark circular patc
his eyes, the bulging neckline, protruding ribs on his chest
sticking out from hands, weary footfalls- all those marks mad
tortured man.

Perhaps the upheaval in 1989 has left no m
impressions in the young minds at present. But the bloodshed ca
the genocide perpetrated could not get wiped out like the dust he
the blinds. Could the history of massacre be replaced by the
digital Chinese euphoria? To me, it would never be possible whate
the government pursue to make it a closed chapter. A crim
always remain a crime and it cannot be washed away by an
goodness or charity. Never and never could it be possible.

My brother died and we couldn't even see his dead b
the misery that follows after his heinous death suffered by us wo
to be carried on till all the leaves of our family tree withered a

ill both of them died with a brunted soul. So in my family
:lung hard and deep inside us that more we tried to shed it off
it became clammy.

Autumn was on the way surrounding us everywhere. Trees
rgreened and flowers such as plum blossoms, peonies, camelias
ritual in full bloom. Winter was yet to pounch upon its cold paw
: we stood with all might to welcome the frigid spectre. Soon
ild be whiteness all around in our rooftops, balconies, roads,
our clothes, hats and upon our eyelids. In winter China thudded
igon that creeps and stays with pain and pleasure. But to us
idn't have a pleasing experience. A bad news arrived but it was
oected at all. We lost another of our family members- my
n the asylum she breathed out last with her anger, cries,
is and also with an unquiet heart. Therapies and medicines
be able to bring her sanity back since Kai had unmade her so
hoped and hoped keeping our fingers crossed in getting her see
and livid. But that didn't happen and when she died alone in that
ve took her death as a salvation from misery. It was an
nious death truly that put an end to our visits to her which had
routine exercise to us. Besides that, it also strengthened me to
hing which my brother Kai had failed to do. But I didn't know
o and the consequence of any misadventure could cost my life.
iother of two kids and a wife of a loving husband I had some
ponsibilities like my father but I didn't want to live like him
j the family ahead of everything.

fiancé and now my husband used to scold me for not having a
hone and he always insisted me to have one for fast
:ating which he to his thinking – the call of the day. But I don't
ve numbers to remember and to transport my likes, dislikes,
ogics everything that I was entwined with. Rather I prefer to
nories that could mystify me, wake me up from deep slumber,
d me like a iron rod, take me way down to the place I left
igo. Memories that I only wish to live with. Some   like green
some became brown nuts and some shapes like withered
to be decayed. Robustly I don't feel the need of social media to
y miseries or my celebrations. Better I would share everything
lose ones who are closer to me always.

stumble or could shake the government at least for a minute. L
the Communist Party would have to shame their faces dow
bloody past- that's what I wanted to do. Silence couldn't be a
at all, I learnt that from my dead brother. Visits to the sq
become a regular exercise to me, looking at the foreigners
continually asking the guides about the tragedy but the fearf
ignore them politely and switch on to other talks. Years
government was still so nervous about it that the people of MS
close watch on the square. People who were earlier tried to do s
obituarily as a mark of respect towards those who were martyr
tragedy were carried away forcibly and swiftly from the square
imprisoned   or killed later. It means that the government
sceptical about it's reputation in this matter and feared to
chances.   The consequences would also be same   if I tri
something for my dead brother but I had to take the risk disreg
what comes about.

It was midnight. Sitting on the bed with a smoke between
was watching my husband lying naked who fucked me an ho
were sleeping tight. After a while I dressed up quickly left
without much noise. Walking down the street I came up to the s
found it almost empty. I had a plan which I had to execute b
vacation ends. During those days I had knocked every newspa
for placing a missing advertisement but everyone turned me
reading the contents of the ad. The people in some newspaper
advised me to give up my plans because a person who went m
thirty years or more could be considered as dead. The ad was
brother Kai who must have been died in the Tiananmen Square
like other martyrs but the body has not been found and so he w
missing since then. It was a missing person's ad. Expected it
like that it didn't surprise me rather I decided to go all by o
printed about hundred copies of the ad from my computer and
secretly behind my bookshelf. If my husband discovered   it
never allow me to make it public the way I intended and that c
about a domestic combat which I did not want either. Kai was m
and why should I put my husband and my kids into such fray.

It was night when slipped out of my bed. With the print

t. The CCTV cameras everwhere around the square should have
ptured my doings. I had completed the task within an hour and
ck to my husband's side where he was still asleep.

s awakened by my husband who was looking at me with his
 and I hugged him down to me and told me " Don't do anything
would not plead guilty." There were footsteps thudding outside
 of my house and I knew who they were and what they came
sed up nicely and greeted them inside. But the officer had told
ey had a warrant against my name and I had to go with them.
rthering the conversation I abided by and went out with them
ck for once, when I saw my husband looking at me helplessly. I
smile at him and went inside the dark van.

n't know where I am now. But the place where I am dungeoned
recisely imprisoned is solitary which helped me to speak to
d to do whatever I feel like. But I don't felt miserable or
of what I had done. There was no remorse in my heart for what
 for my martyred brother. Rather I feel complete and relieved.

****

 some years an inmate was again pulled in inside that prison
 found bold words of democracy on the walls all over which was
tly and fearlessly.

don't know what happened to Shin and where she was taken to
But the words and slogans she had spread inside the walls of
 could illuminate the fearless Chinese who advocates for
 and freedom. The words in Mandarin that defaced the walls
r less translate like this.

" FREEDOM IS NECESSARY TO OUR SURVIVAL OR EL
SURVIVAL BECOMES DEFUNCT".

" RAISE YOUR FISTS TOWARD FREEDOM AND BRING AN
THE COMMUNIST REGIME".

" IF YOU'RE NOT AWARE OF FREEDOM THEN YOU'RE EI
AND WILL AWAYS REMAIN AS A SLAVE"

O COMMUNIST REGIME I HATE IT TILL MY BREATH GOES OFF".

E ONEDAY UNCEREMONIOUSLY BUT I HAVE ALWAYS THE
IN LIVING OF MY OWN".

WHO'RE MARTRYED IN THE TIANANMEN STILL LIVES IN THE
OF MILLIONS OF CHINESE AND IT CANNOT BE COVERED OR
BY THE BRUTE REGIME".

" INFLAME YOURSELF WITH COURAGE THAT COULD BRING DO
REGIME TO YOUR TOES".

" ANY COUNTRY CANNOT MAKE HER COUNTRYMEN HAPPY UNL
UNTIL SHE OFFERED FREEDOM TO THEM- TO MAKE FREE EXC
TO TALK AGAINST UNJUST, TO ELECT THE PEOPLE THEY V
GOVERN ETC."

" FREEDOM SHOULD BE ABSOLUTE AND THERE SHOULD
COMPROMISE IN THIS."

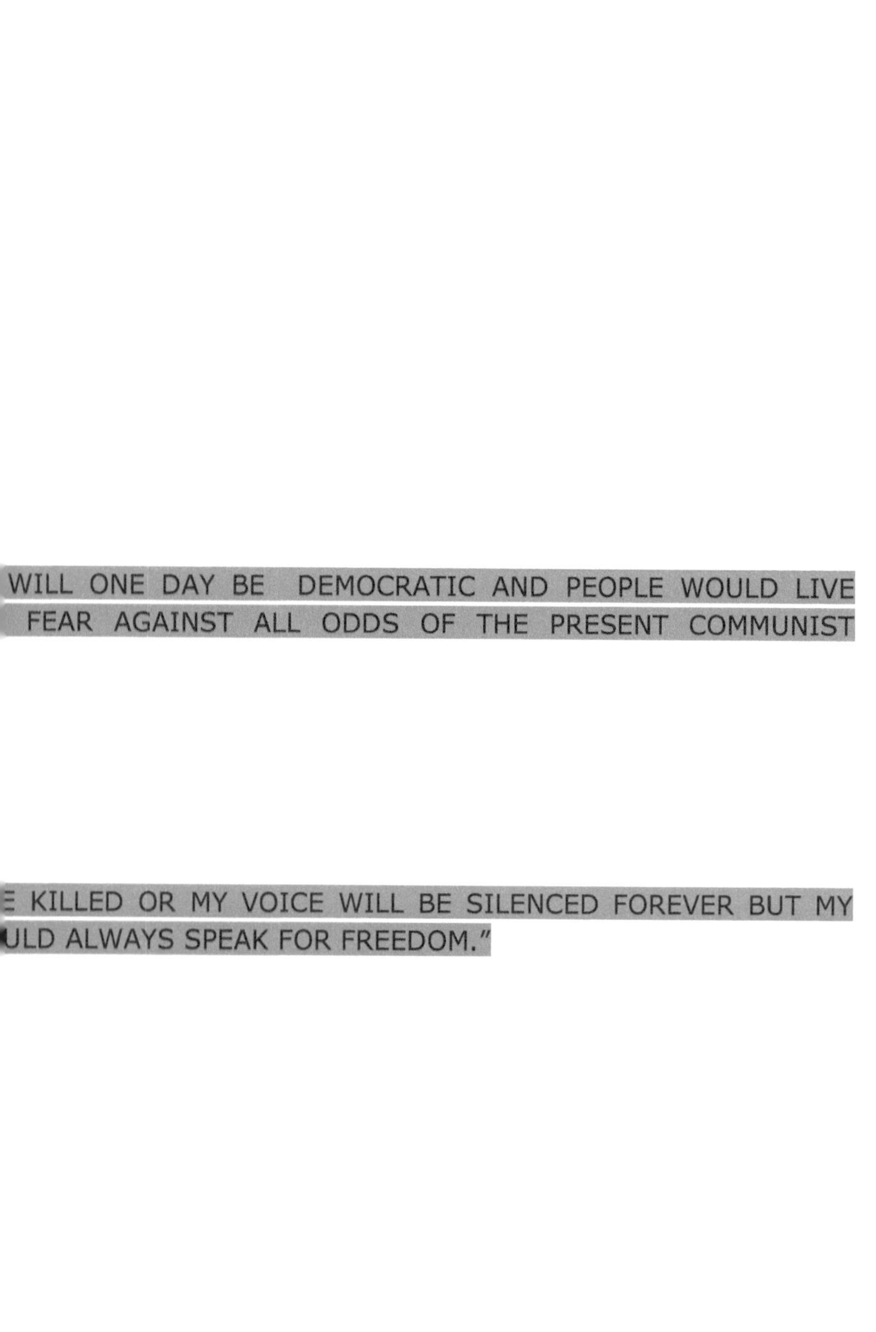
WILL ONE DAY BE DEMOCRATIC AND PEOPLE WOULD LIVE
FEAR AGAINST ALL ODDS OF THE PRESENT COMMUNIST

E KILLED OR MY VOICE WILL BE SILENCED FOREVER BUT MY
ULD ALWAYS SPEAK FOR FREEDOM."